VERMONT

A Picture Book to Remember Her by

CRESCENT BOOKS
NEW YORK

CLB 869
© 1986 Illustrations and text: Colour Library Books Ltd.,
 Guildford, Surrey, England.
Text filmsetting by Acesetters Ltd., Richmond, Surrey, England.
All rights reserved.
1986 edition published by Crescent Books, distributed by Crown Publishers, Inc.
Printed in Spain.
ISBN 0 517 47799 8
h g f e d c b a

One of the toughest trivia questions about the 50 states would be one that asks for the name of the one with the highest rural population. Almost nobody would guess it was Vermont, 66 percent of whose citizens live in rural settings. And it has the country's toughest land use laws that severely restrict ski resorts and shopping malls. Yet it is the 18th most industrialized state.

It is also considered to be one of the most typically "New England" of the New England States, and that makes it all the more attractive to visitors and newcomers. "The qualities of Vermont that were once considered backward are now in vogue," says a state official. "The only reason we have all these lovely old buildings and churches is that nobody had the money to tear them down." "But," adds another, "newcomers pay us the ultimate compliment by trying to imitate us."

It may be that per capita income is lower than in 37 other states, but people migrating there seem to feel that the quality of life in Vermont is a fair tradeoff.

It's a quality of life that hasn't changed much since Colonial times. It has made a typical Vermonter self-reliant, stubborn, independent. They are tolerant and slow to anger, except if someone tries to tell them how to live their lives. And above all, they share a great love for the State of Vermont.

Who can blame them? It's a beautiful place. The three ranges of the Green Mountains come by their name honestly, except in the fall, when their brilliant colors put even the Grand Canyon to shame. There is hardly a barren spot anywhere among its peaks or its notches. The Taconic Mountains along the New York border are gently-rounded and inviting, and form the western boundary of the beautiful Valley of Vermont which merges in the north with the rolling meadows toward the 107-mile-long Lake Champlain. There are more than 400 lakes and ponds in Vermont, and any competition to name the most beautiful of them would surely end up with a hung jury.

Interspersed among it all, the hand of man has created graceful, spired churches and tree-shaded village commons. The countryside is dotted with red barns and pretty white farmhouses, with neatly furrowed fields and peaceful pastures. It has covered bridges and general stores, quaint old inns and a general feeling of traveling back in time to better days.

In spite of an old Vermonter's statement that "A Vermont year is nine months winter and three months of damn poor sleddin'," the climate in Vermont is as delightful as the countryside, though it does get cold in winter, to the delight of skiers up in Killington, Woodstock and other slopes that make it the biggest skiing state east of the Rockies.

Burlington (left) is Vermont's largest city and controls navigation on Lake Champlain. The lighthouse gallery (below) and side-wheeler *S.S. Ticonderoga* (bottom) are two of the interesting exhibits of Shelburne's outdoor museum. Facing page: Vermont has something to offer all year round; skiing takes place at Stowe in winter (bottom), while summer offers walks through rich, green pastures, such as those at farms near Waterbury (top) and Rutland (overleaf), with the tall silos and red barns typical of the area.

The terracotta-colored stone of a church at Pittsford (inset right) is highlighted by the whiteness of Vermont's winter scenery (below and main picture, right). Bottom: a covered bridge typical of New England.

Main picture left and overleaf left: horses graze in the village of Peru, while in the University of Vermont Morgan Horse Farm (inset) are bred the more famous Morgan horses (top and above), the country's oldest, and once most popular, light horse. Overleaf right: a rural scene in the North Landgrove area.

NO FISHING

Equinox Valley Nursery (these pages and overleaf) near Manchester has been run by the same family for three generations and is famous for the 100,000 pounds of pumpkins it produces each fall, as well as other vegetables and berries.

Since the 1930s, when a ski club was founded at Mount Mansfield (top), Stowe (above and facing page bottom) has been the "ski capital of the East." Autumn trees shade a small church in Manchester (left) and Windham Cottage in Grafton (facing page top). Overleaf pages: an aerial view of West Danville and Joe's Pond.

Vermont's famous maple syrup is first extracted as sap from maple trees like those at Quechee Falls (overleaf right), then reduced in sugarhouses, such as the one at Johnson (top right). The moated village of Woodstock (top left) is noted for its fine 18th- and 19th-century houses, which are very different from the modern "frame" house at Stowe (overleaf left). Above: a graveyard in Jericho, under the leaden sky which will soon bring heavy snow to the countryside (left).

Main picture right: the rich colors of a tree-covered hill bring life to a typical winter scene in Vermont. Like Manchester (bottom), Brandon is one of Vermont's many quiet, unspoilt towns, with an interesting collection of 19th-century houses (below and bottom inset) in Federal and Victorian styles. Nestling, as it does, at the foot of the majestic Green Mountain Range, the house (top inset) enjoys a marvellous location. This extension of the Appalachian Chain has given Vermont its name of the Green Mountain State. Overleaf pages: tranquil scenes on the Winooski River near Waterbury.

The massive Rock of Ages quarries at Graniteville in Barre (above and top) have been in operation since 1812 and now produce a third of the country's memorial stones. The arrival of the railroad in 1888 gave impetus to this business by making the quarries accessible to the finishing sheds in outlying areas. The stone is now polished and sculpted at the Craftsmen Centre (inset). Right: Coombs Beaver Brook Sugar House, near Wilmington.

Founded in 1937, Bromley Mountain Ski Resort (these pages) is one of Vermont's oldest ski areas and was among the first to offer such advantages as condominiums, snow farming and snow-making. The mountain commands fine views of Stratton which now owns the resort. One of the state's largest ski resorts is Killington (overleaf left), which boasts the world's largest gondola ski lift. Overleaf right: part of the beautiful scenery north of Rutland.

The old-world atmosphere of the village stores in Marshfields (above, left and below), reflects Vermont's desire to preserve its historical heritage. So, also, does Shelburne Museum, a 45-acre park containing 35 historic buildings brought here from all parts of the state to house a magnificent range of arts and crafts. Among the exhibits, the railway station (below left) recalls the days of the first railroad, brought to Vermont in 1848. Facing page: some of the breathtakingly beautiful scenery in the midst of the Green Mountains.

Bordering beautiful Lake Champlain, Shelburne (this page) is a small, friendly town with a strong sense of the past in the form of many 19th-century farm buildings, as well as its outdoor museum. Facing page top: the State House of the charming capital Montpelier, and (bottom) Vermont College in Burlington. Overleaf pages: the verdant landscape near East Monkton.

Aerial views of the lush pastures of the
Burlington region (top and left) are further
enhanced by a glimpse of Lake Champlain (facing
page), one of America's loveliest lakes. Since its
discovery in 1609 by Samuel de Champlain, it has
been of great historic influence, having been used
by the British as an invasion route during the
War of Independence and again during the War of
1812. Above: a traditional farm near Randolph.

Known as the "Plymouth Notch Historic District," the little town of Plymouth (this page) is noted as the birthplace of Calvin Coolidge, who, from the age of four, lived in the grand house shown (facing page top right) and was inaugurated President of the United States in 1923. Remaining pictures: Woodstock, considered to be one of America's prettiest towns.

Horses (below and top inset) are an important part of the nation's heritage, and rearing and riding them is a feature of the country life that characterises Vermont. An even more potent symbol of its ruralism are the barns and silos of Vermont's scattered farms. The splendid Victorian mansions of Rutland (overleaf) testify to its prosperity in the 19th century, when it was known as the "marble city."

OLD STONE SHOP

Built in 1848, by Batcheller & Sons, makers of pitchforks
⋯
For many years after 1808, farm implements were manufactured here. Lyman Batcheller & his sons bought the forge in 1835, and their forks became famous throughout the U.S. and Europe. In 1902 they merged with the firm making True Temper products, which re-built the Inn.

VERMONT HISTORIC SITES COMMISSION

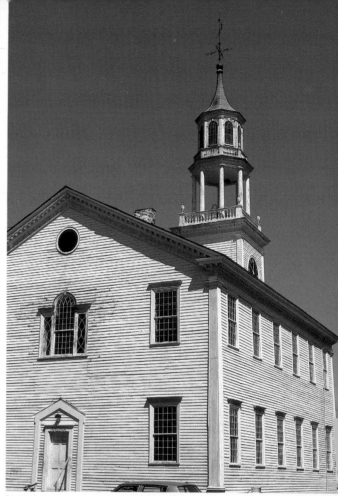

Green Mountain College (above) at Poultney (pictures top, top right and overleaf, bottom right) was the home of Horace Greeley, founder of the *New York Tribune*. Other rural villages include Middletown Springs (right), Wallingford (facing page), and Pawlet (overleaf right, top). Overleaf left: Dorset (bottom right), Townsend (top right) and Bennington (remaining pictures), with its battle monument and old graveyard.

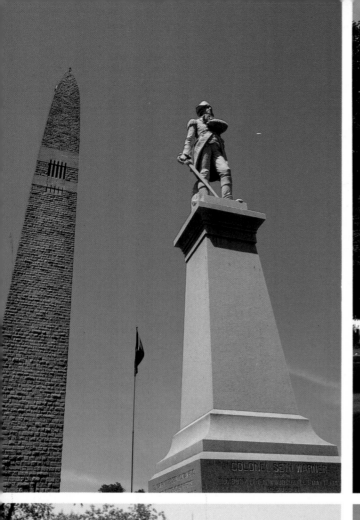

In some forgotten, deserted woodland are found an abandoned car and a derelict shed (below). More typical of Vermont's picturesque country life is the farmhouse sheltered by hills (top inset), the roadside post boxes of a small community (bottom), the Middlebury River rushing through the trees at Ripton (main picture right) and a traditional covered bridge at the Shelburne Museum (bottom inset). Overleaf: the colors of awakening nature begin to appear as the snow melts from the landscape near Rutland (left) and Warren (right).

By the 1940s the Old Tavern of Grafton (left) – which in the 1800s had been a thriving, celebrity-filled inn – had begun to join in the decline of the rest of the village (remaining pictures). However, the next few decades saw the renovation of Grafton thanks to the inheritance money of Hall and Dean, who expanded the tavern and funded several projects, including a museum, a nursery and even a cheese factory.

Vermont's fall (these pages) has become
something of an institution; from the end
of September onwards reports on color
progress are issued weekly, foliage counts
are taken and festivals are held to
celebrate this lovely, colorful season.
Dappled sunlight falls on a golden carpet
of leaves in Woodstock (right), which is
noted for its beautiful, old houses and was
the home of many celebrities, one of whom,
Senator Jacob Collamer (1791-1865), said
"the good people of Woodstock have less
incentive than others to yearn for
heaven." From above, the colors of the
land between Morrisville and St. Johnsbury
(overleaf) make a rich pattern.